Marsh Morning

By Marianne Berkes

Illustrated by
Robert Noreika

The Millbrook Press
Brookfield, Connecticut

For Emily Anne,
our own little songbird!
MSB

To Chris, Sarah and my mother.
RN

Library of Congress Cataloging-in-Publication Data
Berkes, Marianne Collins.
Marsh morning / Marianne Berkes ; illustrated by Robert Noreika.
p. cm.
Includes bibliographical references (p.   ).
Summary: Beginning with the first light of dawn, the marsh comes alive with music as different
types of birds tune up and perform nature's symphony.
ISBN 0-7613-2568-9 (lib. bdg.)   ISBN 0-7613-1936-0 (trade)
1. Birdsongs—Juvenile literature. [1. Birdsongs. 2. Songbirds.]
I. Noreika, Robert, ill. II. Title.
QL698.5 .B49 2003   598.159'4—dc21   2001008464

Published by The Millbrook Press, Inc.
2 Old New Milford Road
Brookfield, Connecticut 06804
www.millbrook press.com

Wings of color fill the sky
A happy Song, a joyful Cry.
Spirits lift, old Dreams Renew.
When Birds take wing,
Our Hearts soar Too.
Anonymous

The moon is gone; dawn is breaking.
Soon the songbirds will be waking.

A rabbit peeks out from his hole.
He hops upon the mound,
Where frogs convened to fill the night
With cacophonic sound.

Now it's still in the marshy cove.
The rabbit hops away.
Where are the sounds the morning makes
As night turns into day?

Great Blue Heron

As dawn appears, a heron stands
Motionless offshore.
He spears a fish and gulps it down
And waits to get some more.

Then the first song:—*o-ka-leee*—
The blackbird starts his melody.
A red-bellied woodpecker *chucks* away
As birds begin to greet the day.

American
Bittern

Red-winged Blackbird

Common Yellowthroat

The dawn chorus swells up in the marsh;
Some sounds are sweet and others harsh.
Oon-KA-chunk, caw, tweet, twit—
"Witchity-witchity-witchity-wit."

Red-bellied
Woodpecker

Song Sparrow

Marsh Wren

A sparrow trills an aria;
Two wrens sing a duet.
Eight blackbirds nesting in the reeds
Perform a loud octet.

Sandhill cranes flock to the pond.
The flapping of their wings
Adds to the sound the sparrow makes
As on and on he sings.

Sandhill Crane

The day's awake now with this prattle;
The cranes sing loud and low.
They bow to their partners, shake and rattle,
And then they *do-si-do*!

More cranes fly in to join the flock;
The rhythm really starts to rock.
Woodpecker's drumming out a beat
As cranes keep moving with their feet.

Mourning
Dove

Common Snipe

The chorus does more vocalizing.
The beat is off—that's not surprising!
Ragtime music's in the air.
You can't escape; it's everywhere.

Birds are in communication.
Can you hear the syncopation?
Whu, whu, whu, whu, whu
Coo-ah, coo, coo, coo.

Mallards

Most of the birds have had their lunch
When dabbling ducks come in a bunch,
Flying in a V-formation
Quacking with anticipation.

Looks like a pretty good place to stop.
They land on the water with a plop.
Tails in the air, down they go,
To eat vegetation that grows below.

Then they parade along the shore;
The ducks want to look around some more.
One, two—feel the beat.
They waddle along on marching feet.

Tree Swallows

Swallows are chanting *twit, twit, twit*.
They are doing their own little skit.
Zooming around in the afternoon sky
Catching insects on the fly.

Common Moorhen

There's more entertainment down below.
A moorhen does a one-bird show.
While swallows above are *twitting* nonstop
The chicken-like bird is doing bebop.

The day is coming to an end:
Look at the blushing sky.
A flock of ibis sails with the wind.
How gracefully they fly!

White Ibis

They pump down low across the pond,
Then high up in the trees they land.
As day turns into night again
They're sleeping as they stand.

Common Loon

Not over yet; there's one more tune:
The tremolo of a laughing loon.
Ha-oo-oo he sings as he takes flight.
Where is the music of the night?

The birds in the marsh have gone to sleep.
Look over on the log
Gronk, gronk; pe-ep peep peep
I think I hear . . .

A frog!

Aria (a´ re a)—a song, a solo in an opera that stands by itself.

Beat (beet)—the time it takes to tap your foot once.

Bebop (bee´ bop)—a sharp distinctive two-tone phrase in jazz music.

Cacophonic (ka kaf´o nik)—harsh, noisy sounds.

Chant (chant)—a repetitive song or melody.

Chorus (kor´es)—a group of singers.

Do-si-do (do´ ze do)—a movement in folk dancing.

Duet (doo et´)—music for two voices.

March (march)—to walk with steady steps of equal length.

Melody (mel´ o de)—pleasing sounds in sequence.

Octet (ak tet´)—music for eight voices.

Ragtime (rag´ tim)—music characterized by strong syncopation in even time.

Rhythm (rith´ em)—measured motion; a flow of movement.

Syncopation (sin´ ke pa´ shen)—beginning a tune on an unaccented beat.

Tremolo (trem´ e lo)—a quivering effect produced by rapid repetition of the same tone.

Trill (tril)—the quick alternation of two adjacent notes.

Vocalize (vo´ kel iz´)—a singing exercise.

The Cast

Great Blue Heron (up to 4 feet, 122 cm). A slow, methodical stalker, this wading bird looks for fish or frogs with its head hunched on its shoulders. In flight, its neck is folded into an S-curve. A majestic flyer, the heron can reach speeds of 30 miles (48 km) per hour. Usually silent, it sometimes calls with a hoarse squawk.

Red-winged Blackbird (7–10 inches, 18–25 cm). The black male has bright red shoulder patches, which are displayed during his "song spread." Often perched on a cattail, he spreads his wings and tail as he sings. One of the most common and familiar wetland birds, his rich musical *o-ka-leee* is usually the first sound of the new day.

Red-bellied Woodpecker (10 inches, 25 cm). This woodpecker is common in Southeastern woodlands and also seen in swampy marshlands where there are trees in which to excavate a new home. He has a red crown and also a reddish patch on his lower abdomen. His voice is a *chuck-chuck-chuck* descending in pitch.

American Bittern (23–34 inches, 58–86 cm). When approached, the bittern freezes and blends in with the landscape, its bill thrust skyward. This shy bird is more likely to be heard than seen. His mating call can be heard a half-mile away. His croak, which has led to his nickname "thunder-pumper," is *oon-KA-chunk*.

Common Yellowthroat (4½–6 inches, 11.5–15 cm) This tiny bird can be spotted by color and call. It likes to nest near water, in swamps and grassy marshes. The male can be quite conspicuous, as he perches on the tip of a cattail singing with all his might. His voice is a fast *witchity-witchity-witchity-wit*.

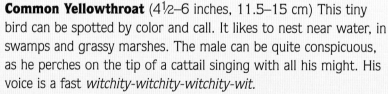

Song Sparrow (5½–7 inches, 14–18 cm). This bird is found almost everywhere in North America. It is brown with grayish streaks; its tail is usually reddish brown. Its song has three sweet notes followed by a varied trill, sometimes interpreted as *Madge-Madge-Madge, put-on-your-tea-kettle-ettle-ettle*.

Marsh Wren (4–5½ inches, 10–14 cm). Brown with a white streaked back and a distinct white stripe over the eye, the marsh wren nests in reeds, cattails, and tall marsh grasses. This small noisy bird begins his song with a few scraping notes followed by a gurgling sound that ends with a musical trill.

Sandhill Crane (34–48 inches, 86–122 cm). Mostly gray in color, with a red forehead. Unlike herons, cranes fly with their long necks outstretched. On land, they use their long legs to leap into the air with their wings extended, doing their mating dance. Facing each other, they bow and jump, calling with a low, loud rattle.

Common Snipe (10½ inches, 27 cm). A brownish shorebird with a very long bill and striped head. The snipe's zigzag flight is fast and erratic, especially when it is flushed from the edge of a pond or marsh. From high over the marsh, it flutters its tail feathers, making a sound like *whu, whu, whu, whu, whu.*

Mourning Dove (12 inches, 30 cm). This abundant pigeon-like bird is common in all parts of the United States. A soft sandy-brown color, its head is small. The mourning dove has black spots on its wings, and its long-pointed tail is edged with white. The sad notes of this bird's song are first heard at dawn: *Coo-ah, coo, coo, coo.*

Mallard (18–27 inches, 46–69 cm). This duck is a dabbling duck; it stays on the surface of the water, tipping its tail, putting its head under to find food. It is the most abundant duck in the world. The male mallard has a beautiful green head, chestnut breast and grayish body. He utters a soft, reedy note, while the female make a loud *quack.*

Tree Swallow (5–6¼ inches, 13–16 cm). Very graceful in the air, swallows gather in enormous flocks along the Atlantic Coast in the fall. The tree swallow is a common nester in tree cavities, especially near water. It has a metallic blue or blue-green back, while the throat and breast are white. Its voice is a continuous series of twits and chatters.

Common Moorhen (13 inches, 33 cm). With long and webless toes, this chicken-like bird strides over floating plants, like lily pads, even in the deepest parts of the marsh. It constantly bobs its head while swimming or walking. When it takes off in flight, it runs across the water at a frantic pace until airborne. It is a friendly bird that cackles like a hen.

White Ibis (23–27 inches, 58–69 cm). These wading birds are long legged and very graceful. At dusk, as they get ready to roost, they come pumping across the water, often set against the brilliance of the setting sun. Long lines of birds stream from all directions. They land in trees and bushes and stand silently as night falls. Their voice is a grunt or growl.

Common Loon (28–36 inches, 71–91 cm). A large duck-like waterbird with a thick, pointy bill. The loon dives with ease and can swim long distances underwater, but is clumsy on land. It spends its life eating and sleeping on open water and migrates at night. You can hear the loon's yodel-like laugh when it is in flight: *ha, ha, ha, ha; hoo, hoo, hoo; ha-oo-oo.*

Bibliography

Audubon Society. *Familiar Birds of North America* (Western Region). New York: Alfred A. Knopf, 1986.

Bansemer, Roger with Bill Renc. *At Water's Edge: The Birds of Florida.* Dallas, TX: Taylor Publishing, 1993.

Eastman, John. *Birds of Lake, Pond and Marsh.* Mechanicsburg, PA: Stackpole Books, 1999.

National Audubon Society. *Field Guide to North American Birds* (Eastern Region). New York: Alfred A. Knopf, 1998.

Schinkel, Dick. *Favorite Birds of Florida.* Holt, MI: Thunder Bay Press, 1995.

Thompson III, Bill. *Bird Watching for Dummies.* Foster City, CA: IDG Books Worldwide, 1997.